CLIMBING THE DIVIDE

CLIMBING
THE DIVIDE

WALT McDONALD

UNIVERSITY OF NOTRE DAME PRESS
Notre Dame, Indiana

Published by the University of Notre Dame Press
Notre Dame, Indiana 46556
www.undpress.nd.edu
All Rights Reserved

Manufactured in the United States of America

Library of Congress Cataloging-in-Publication Data

McDonald, Walter.
Climbing the divide / Walt McDonald.
p.   cm.
ISBN 0-268-02280-1 (cloth : alk. paper)
ISBN 0-268-02281-X (pbk. : alk. paper)
I. Title.
PS3563.A2914 C58   2003
813'.54—dc21
2002156583

Contents

3. TAKING THE KEYS AWAY

4. OCTOBER COMPOST

5. OUT PAST THE BREAKERS

Acknowledgments

I'm deeply grateful to editors of the following publications in which earlier versions of these poems first appeared, some with different titles:

Acre:
"When I Glance Up"

Adirondack Review:
"Blizzards When I Was Ten"

American Scholar:
"Hosanna in the Family"

Appalachia:
"A Fed Bear Is a Dead Bear"
"Dazzling Montana Dawns"

Bellowing Ark:
"Praise"

Christian Century:
"After His Apache Crashed"
"On the Porch Swing at Dawn"
"The War in Bosnia, the Beach at Kitty Hawk"
"This Could Be Eden"

Christianity and Literature:
"Before Flying Off to War"
"The Dark, Hollow Halo of Space"

Clackamas Literary Review:
"Fencing the Hardpan"

Concho River Review:
"Stranded in Snowpacked Mountains"

Connecticut Review:
"The Summer Uncle Carl's Herd Was Sold"

Dalhousie Review (Canada):
"Angelica's Banjo and Karate"

Drunken Boat:
"A Little World Made Cunningly"
"Doctors, Lawyers, Undertakers"

Electronic Poetry Review:
"Hiking Grizzly Country with Bells"
"The Rockies, Tooth and Claw"
"What God Felt Like When I Was Twelve"

Ellipsis: Literature and Art:
"Cascading down McDonald Creek"

Envoi (U.K.):
"Clouds Whip By in the Valley"

Gettysburg Review:
"Driving at Night across Texas"

First Things:
"Giving Time to the Dirt in Rows"

JAMA: The Journal of the American Medical Association:
"The Blocks Grandfather Carved"
"Climbing the Divide in Montana" (with another title;
     also in *Notre Dame Review*)
"Finding My Father's Hands in Midlife"
"Months of Butterrum"
"My Father Light as a Boy"

"Old Men Are Dreamers"
"Some Days Nothing Can Save Us"
"Taking the Keys Away"
"Words I Looked Up in World War Two"

Listening Eye:
"The Year Biology Made Sense"

Literature and Belief:
"Island Hopping with MacArthur"

Midwest Quarterly:
"A Clown Fired from a Cannon"
"That Night and Others Like It"

Missouri Review:
"Uncle Bob and the Art of Taxidermy"

New York Review of Books:
"Squall Line at Sixty-Five"

North American Review:
"After the Mad Songs of Saigon"

North Dakota Quarterly:
"The Winter of Desert Storm"

Notre Dame Review:
"Climbing the Divide in Montana"
    (with another title; also in *JAMA*)

Orion:
"A Brief Familiar Story of Winter"

Ontario Review:
"Boys on Winter Palominos"
"Grandmother's Thousand Cats"

Open Spaces:
"After Fires in Montana"

Oxford American:
"Jogging at Sixty-Five"

Paumanok Review:
"Downhill to Granddaddy's Barn"

Pennsylvania English:
"Town Girls When I Was Nine"

Perspectives:
"Magical Hammocks at Bedtime"

Ploughshares:
"Black as the Plains Out There"

Poet Lore:
"Packing Parachutes in Flight School"

Prairie Schooner:
"Stumbling to the Deck at Dawn"
"With My Son's Bow at Dusk"

Rattle:
"Breathless for Twenty Seconds"

Seattle Review:
"That Clatter in the Attic"
"Uncle Earl's Last Ride in Dallas"

Southwest Review:
"The Gulls of Kitty Hawk"

Trouvere:
"Fog on the Outer Banks"

U.S. Catholic:
"My Wife's First Day of Class"

Westview:
"Stoking the Logs"

Witness:
"Bless Weeds That Bloom in Fall"

———

"Hosanna in the Family" is reprinted from *The American Scholar,* Volume 60, Number 3, 2000. Copyright 2000 by Walter McDonald.

"The Blocks Grandfather Carved." *JAMA: The Journal of the American Medical Association* 284.19 (2000): 2424. Copyright 2000, American Medical Association.

"Finding My Father's Hands in Midlife." *JAMA: The Journal of the American Medical Association* 285.2 (2001): 142. Copyright 2001, American Medical Association.

"Months of Butterrum." *JAMA: The Journal of the American Medical Association* 287.10 (2002): 2228. Copyright 2002, American Medical Association.

"My Father Light as a Boy." *JAMA: The Journal of the American Medical Association* 286.4 (2001): 390. Copyright 2001, American Medical Association.

"Old Men Are Dreamers." *JAMA: The Journal of the American Medical Association* 284.13 (2000): 1625. Copyright 2000, American Medical Association.

"Some Days Nothing Can Save Us." *JAMA: The Journal of the American Medical Association* 285.9 (2001): 1128. Copyright 2001, American Medical Association.

Acknowledgments | xiii

CLIMBING THE DIVIDE

PART 1

Breathless for Twenty Seconds

When I Glance Up

Buckets swing and jingle against her knees.
I could hobble out and help, but who'd do the math—
so many calves, so many bushels an acre,
so many days before it rains.

When I glance up, she's on the slope
going slow, moccasins swishing in grass
down to the spring. My hip has itched
all week, fire from knee to the groin.

I slide a bent wire hanger down
inside the cast, scratch what I can reach
like a dog in winter clawing fleas,
coat too thick to nip them with his teeth.

I need to hang storm windows
before the blizzards come, and patch the roof,
my hammer there where I left it, clumsy,
falling like a tumbling act without a net.

We said if we build here, water would run
always cool, the chimney would draw,
the roof swirled free of smog, no honking cars,
no telephones. And now she's back,

hardly huffing, big buckets bumping,
ripples splashing the path from both pails,
lips parted and licked till they glisten,
a shimmer of sweat on her cheeks.

With My Son's Bow at Dusk

I call and hear a thistle flick the house.
Another weed I missed, too busy to take time.
My son comes running with his bow,

empty quiver flouncing on his back.
Whatever he shot in the arbor he missed,
maybe pears too green to pick. The full moon

bulges, and next day's lessons wait.
Tomorrow we'll hunt the arrows,
and I'll say again don't shoot

unless he can follow the feathers
and find them. Tousle-haired and eight,
he hands me the bow and runs,

and the backdoor slams. I almost call,
but I'm eight again myself, and lift the bow
and aim, pretending, string taut

and tingling in my tips, the arbor dark,
one shadow darker and gobbling,
one last fat turkey I can't miss.

Hosanna in the Family

Uncle Earl rolled his eyes over Aunt Bernice
and winked. Aunt Bernice was a honey,
curvy and plump. Earl deeded her parents
a section of his ranch, a dowry she didn't have,

sweetheart so well endowed he didn't mind,
would have signed his sunburned soul
on the dotted line. Before Vietnam,
before my cousin Bobby died at Da Nang,

I worked eight summers on the ranch,
their only nephew. Uncle Earl taught us
to ride, to rope and hold a calf down
for branding, to jab and burn its hide

and step back while it flounced and rose.
Aunt Bernice heaped biscuits on our plates,
and yellow butter, my cousin's creamy mother
who worshiped sunburned Uncle Earl,

who drawled raw jokes and stabbed his fork
in the air like pitching hay. What simple days
before the war, hard work and horses
I thought I'd ride forever with Bobby,

Aunt Bernice spoiling us all, forking sausage
and biscuits on our plates, winking
at Bobby and me, leaning toward Uncle Earl
and humming, patting his big-boned fists.

Driving at Night across Texas

Her arms held all the songs I longed for,
and four tires took me there.
I was a pilot at a base on the border,
more time on the highway than flying,
driving at night across Texas,

humming all the old songs.
But we keep losing our heroes,
grandparents and singers, friends
missing in action. Car wrecks take them away,
or drugs, planes that crash in mountains

or winter fields, or plain old death.
I think of Glenn Miller in World War Two,
Patsy Cline and Billie Holiday, and a boy
from my hometown named Buddy Holly.
Seven grandchildren after a war,

Vietnam is always a fact—*there it is,*
even in dreams. Some go on
in hospital beds or wheelchairs,
some so boldly brave I'm stunned.
I rock with my wife under stars

on the lawn swing, stroking the same hair
dark as it was those nights in Austin
when the world seemed like a bandstand
and we had coins enough forever,
the jukebox full of songs.

Grandmother's Thousand Cats

Grandmother majored in French and Latin
and raised cats. She numbered them,
digits in the French tongue lovely,
and they purred. After Grandfather's horse

tossed him off in a storm, she taught college,
the oldest bachelor of arts on the faculty.
Her students liked her cats, learned French
by riding to the ranch for practice,

counting her cats *deux, trois,* and grooming mares.
My mother met my father there, branding calves
for his mother, the ranch Grandmother
left them, cats and a thousand cows.

Mother teased she taught him the tongue
so he'd feed kittens, more than a hundred
when I was born. He let them prowl, squeezed
milk to their mouths from teats of cows.

When my children were toddlers, he lined them up
like cats in the barn, tongues out,
giggling and squinting, my father
squeezing warm streams to them all.

Breathless for Twenty Seconds

She's leaning away in the film
and listening to herself,
humming to music we can't hear.

Last month, we leaned by her bed
and hardly breathed. Whatever
our mother tried to tell us

that last hour before she died,
we'll never know. This movie of her
and Father before the war

has no sound, so old it's brittle.
Inches of film snap off each time
we load it and the sprockets turn.

My God! she was lovely, our father
breathless for twenty seconds,
her hair glossy dark, her body shapely

before children, any of us.
Father's not in most rolls,
but came back from the war

without a scratch, only night sweats,
battles he never shared.
He took this film at Christmas—

look how the focus stays on our mother,
who didn't know he filmed her
on a ladder, hanging mistletoe.

Someone probably called, or laughter
turned her around. Look at that—
surprised, delighted, she mouths

our father's name, her long skirt sways,
the ladder shaky—but now, the film
is blank spots blinking by,

then nothing but the screen's
bright light, the plastic clicking
until I flick the switch.

Magical Hammocks at Bedtime

Ever the weaver, my wife taught
my gawky hands to hold babies like yarn
while she treadled and bedded them down
after bottles and baths. Dressed them

and blessed them, lady who watched them
in sickness and health, in a cradle shaped
like a loom. She taught them to waddle
to swings after playpens, pulled them

till autumn in wagons, then sleds
across lakes where trucks drove
loaded with stones. Bedtime, she told
about shepherds and wise men and stars,

boys with slingshots and harps,
weaving magical hammocks at bedtime.
They're grown now and *poof!* they're gone,
and our house is a loom. I'm stiff-thumbed,

clumsy, our garden a jungle, oaks brittle
for cracking if winter storms bring ice.
She's white-haired and weaving, bent over
shawls and granddaughters' doll clothes.

She twinkles, twenty in every way
but age, massager of shoulders and neck
when I'm weary, beside me at night
on the sofa, watching the oak logs blaze.

Cascading down McDonald Creek

Clouds entangle us in snowcapped mountains
bulging above us. Heads back, we revel
and we stare. Clouds rise and clash,

should echo back like boulders.
How can such vapor swirls keep silence?
The Lord's in His holy temple, here,

even though signs in Glacier Park warn
Here there be grizzlies. Plaques along park roads
explain the fossils, plate tectonics.

A month in Glacier Park's a blink,
a glimpse of switchbacks, a million rocks
not even scratched. Nights under blankets,

we lie with curtains wide and watch the stars.
Hiking, we lean over thousands of feet
where trickles start, tumbling to a stream

we've picnicked by, cascading down McDonald Creek,
to rivers, the Pacific, back as snow
over glaciers, high in hosanna clouds.

This Could Be Eden

So blue a jet would slice a contrail
like a diamond, snapping the sky in half.
Rocky mountains so green it seems

they could never burn. Hard granite
to hold the world together forever.
From this, no one would guess

a grizzly mangled a hiker at dawn,
ripped off her face and chest,
the raw heart stopped when they found her.

Who could intuit lava underground,
the bubbling rocks we walk on?
On this calm day, who could imagine wars,

heartache, or cancer, without telegrams
or cell phones? Here on this
almost perfect day, on the deck

of a mountain cabin, we rock,
talk softly although we haven't heard
a door or seen another soul since dawn.

Except for that tragic news report,
this could be Eden.
Except for grandchildren we adore,

far off on the continent,
in school by now, guards in the halls,
classmates with books and satchels,

some with dustcoats
over grudges no one knows,
but burning to show the world.

A Fed Bear Is a Dead Bear

Bears waddle off, glancing back
at tourists who ignore signs
posted on every road—*Don't feed the bears,
If bears come by, stay in your cars.*
Feed bears today, park rangers warn,
we'll have to kill them, tomorrow,

spoiled by the soft touch of tourists,
and hungry. Any hour, let sightseers
glimpse a bear in bushes by the road—
holding his toes and swaying on his butt
to beg, or munching huckleberries—
there's gridlock, cars for a hundred yards

stopped at all angles on the asphalt,
drivers with cameras and snacks hopping out,
flagging down oncoming cars, *Look,
look.* Sometimes, even a grizzly turns,
stares hard at scraps and biscuits pitched,
and bows her massive back.

Stranded in Snowpacked Mountains

Today I'm crazy for prairie, stranded
in snowpacked mountains with cliffs and columbine.
Any flat range would do, guiding a gelding away
from the barn. No oats, today, not yet.

I'm mad for rattlers and cactus, cougars sleeping it off,
hawks caught spiraling higher in thermals.
If the sorrel aimed for a fence, I'd snip it,
enough barbed wire to mend it later when I was sane.

If Joe or Billy Ray rode by, I'd tip back my hat
and stop. We'd swap dry facts about mares and cows,
how many colts and calves, how many died.
We'd slap leather like bandits and blast a stump

full of holes. We wouldn't keep score.
Other old vets might hear us and call, cell phones
like locusts buzzing across a dozen miles.
Loping, they'd find us lazy and lost

like a posse, far from wives and the war,
the sun so dry we burned. If there was a shade,
we'd all dismount and squat, tip Stetsons back
and take turns telling jokes. Dusk,

or when nobody laughed anymore, someone would say
There it is, and we'd rock longer on our heels
till the shade's all gone, or one of us
straightened up and said *It's dinner time.*

Climbing the Divide in Montana

Stub of a month, so many crags and valleys
and nothing but old legs to climb them.
Light as moleskin, even our boots are cracked,
backpacks stitched again, again. Loaded

and hoisted up, they snug the small of our backs
like hands we know and never tire of.
We don't throw away old gear because it's brittle.
We've come two thousand miles for wild Montana.

Tomorrow, we'll go back to cattle neighbors watch,
to debts and telephone. Even after fifty years
of coming here, we're giddy, tongue-tied
like on our honeymoon, babbling but panting now,

stopping more often, binoculars wobbling
as we stare past fir and aspen, sweeping past
snowcapped timberline, always another cave
in a cliff. Who could live here all year?

Dazzled, we're out of breath.
Even a million acres of huckleberries
still taste sour. Give us a week, another month,
let them ripen. We might find dozens of bighorn sheep

nibbling tundra, another grizzly rising up
a thousand yards uphill to sniff and stare,
maybe a cougar hungry under a ledge of shale,
blinking, flicking its dark-tipped tail.

Praise

It's four, Montana cabin cold.
I lift a blanket past her arms
and slip outside with coffee,
valley so still I hear the Amtrak
to Seattle miles away. No breeze
or stars, the deck so cold

steam rises like a rope trick
from the cup. The moon plays poker
with a deck of clouds, and folds.
Last week, a pack of wolves downwind
raised muzzles to the moon and howled,
prowlers of mountains back in Montana.

Praise dark before the dawn.
Praise God who made the dawn
and water tumbling down from snow,
the tap I'll turn today. Praise God
for sleep, for grizzlies
wild in the mountains, and massive.

For breath that puffs away,
for this dark day, the sun
we're spinning around, the moon
I believe is out there past the clouds.
For my wife's closed eyes
I need to open once more, soon.

PART 2

The Year Biology Made Sense

Boys on Winter Palominos

We sharpened icicles like assassins,
milking the tips like teats to make them melt,
sculpting ice daggers with our hands
until they ached. Grandfather's leaky barn
dripped like a grotto in blizzards,

cows' heat melting the snow to ice.
The dark loft dangled stalactites
five feet long and thicker than our necks.
Most crashed to the floor when we whacked them,
but the best made lances, so heavy

we staggered. Daggers strapped to our coats,
Eddy and I galloped around the corral
on imaginary palominos, cousins
hugging the butts of lances longer than us,
Quixotes before we had heard the word.

Our brothers were off on battleships
or islands in World War Two, but we were boys
with movie ranches to rescue. Most icicles broke
when we stumbled, or jabbed them hard
at the barn to get at the bad men,

bank robbers barricaded, whiskey-drunk
on rotgut and firing wildly. When lances broke,
we dropped them and charged the barn,
grabbing slippery knives and whooping like savages,
leaping at shadows crouched behind the stalls.

The Summer Uncle Carl's Herd Was Sold

Knuckles battered by bulls,
Uncle Carl locked the paddock
and leaped back, dusting his pants

with both gloves. Buzzards kissed his calves
goodbye when he rode off, keeping watch
on cattle in drought, stray calves

in a valley of coyotes. My sister and I
loved that bearded old man, bowlegged
and bald. When we rode his colts

and stayed on, his growl
was the praise we worked for.
When we fell, his cigar bobbing smoke

told us both *No worry*. One month
when his gelding tumbled, only buzzards
soared to his rescue. We were in school

miles away from that canyon.
Calves bawled and wandered off
from his broken back, no one to hear

Uncle Carl groan, or the rifle
he kept firing for help
after his gelding died.

Town Girls When I Was Nine

Street kids envied our ponies,
how we trotted to town from the ranch,
the horses we rode every day
over many miles on the plains.
New kids in town when our one-room
ranch school closed, I let them stroke

and talk to the gelding, then rode
to the stable and left him
and ran to catch up with my brother,
to the school two blocks away.
My brother envied their bikes,
the store-bought cigars they swiped.

He envied their daddies who kept boxes
of cigars in their homes, didn't miss
what their spoiled kids sneaked.
Joe was older than me by a year,
and I didn't smoke after cigars
of willow bark we crushed

and rolled in toilet paper and lit.
What I liked about Eddy and Earl
and their gang was what they could see
any day, even weekends—twenty girls
in a flat town of a thousand,
the magic of brunettes and blondes,

pretty classmates we met that first day
who rocked in their seats
and watched us like mavericks,
batting their eyes and flirting
over tiny, up-lifted shoulders
before the teacher made them turn.

The Year Biology Made Sense

When brunette Trudy moved to town,
we boys in fourth grade saw
what biology was for. We'd heard,

but sullen girls were nothing to us
but skinny kids who rolled their eyes
and made good grades. They whispered a lot

and wept and never played our games.
But sleepy-eyed Trudy came in April,
near the end of school, and all she taught

we learned. To watch her cross the room
was college. Trudy was curves and honey,
the show-and-tell for well-thumbed magazines

big brothers hid, and cars we found
abandoned at the park. Then, theology
and math made sense, the parables

of puppy love and Oz. When Trudy
bent her dimpled knees and tucked
to sit down at her desk, we spoke in tongues.

Doctors, Lawyers, Undertakers

Sue said we couldn't tell turtles from knuckles
in soup. She worked with worms,
turned fifth-grade girls and boys

away from baseball and hopscotch
to biology. See that? she asked
and stepped back from the microscope,

so we, lined up, could look—
a bit of tissue from inside her lip
displayed naked on the stage.

That's how we look to worms,
she confessed, sticky cell fiber,
tasty enough to eat.

Sue patted us on the back
and looked us in the eye,
examining our brows, the shape

of our gritted jaws and skulls,
forecasting our futures.
She made us call her Sue,

our teacher in love with flesh
and the leveler worm, even us—
some of us peeking *Wow!* into worlds

of microscopes and slides,
some flipping fingertips
when they backed away,

not knowing what to say
with pinched or puckered lips,
some simply green.

Island Hopping with MacArthur

My father loved MacArthur, and why not?
his middle son a prisoner on Luzon,
if he survived the death march from Bataan.
Often my father stared at the pin
he called Australia, the General's pin,

inches from where my brother's was.
I tried to spin the globe
but he caught my wrist in his fist
as if I'd whirl my brother off the world.
I was six, and ran to friends and baseball,

forgot my brother and the nightly news.
At meals, my father prayed *MacArthur,*
and my mother nodded. Then I was nine
with a Babe Ruth bat, and the radio said
he sailed back with a thousand ships

to liberate *his boys.* When he waded ashore—
striding head-high, captured by a cameraman—
my father wept. *People of the Philippines,*
the far-off voice came scratchy on the radio—
I have returned. Years later, I heard

when the General set survivors free,
when he took my starving brother
by both shoulders, my starving brother
could hardly whisper, *You came back—*
and MacArthur nodded like a God, like Father.

Blizzards When I Was Ten

Cattle would freeze before dawn, without help,
so Father rode out while it was night.
Sinking deep in snow by the porch, his boots
said fifteen inches, but maybe that was drifts.

Drifts stacked deeper by the fence
where steers wandered and stopped,
hundreds mashed against barbed wire,
too dumb and cold to break it down.

He knew how far to the neighbor's grove,
how many wires he'd have to cut
if he could find the herd, snow-coated lumps by now.
Yes, he came back by noon, yes, most steers

drifted downwind to the grove and stopped. Both storms,
while Father lost four toes and forty steers,
I slept downstairs by the fire he built.
Oh, I tried watching till sunrise while he rode

and even prayed for him, to be a man like him,
but slept in Daddy's chair under quilts
Grandmother spread—a boy, after all,
who couldn't stay awake one hour.

The Blocks Grandfather Carved

Hawk or a grizzly's head, Grandfather's oak
curled up and toppled. Every scrape, every plane
of the wood clamped tightly in the vise
might be his last. And so old knuckles

the size of walnuts made a fist that trembled,
pain I never understood until lately,
when I bend to pick a grandchild up.
One day I watched him hold the blade

and wait until the tremor stopped,
then strop the sharp steel deep enough in oak
to cut a jaw. I saw a bear's jaw drop,
and fangs grew out of wood, the muzzle dished,

a grizzly. I saw the ears perk up to listen.
It sits there on the mantel now, without eyes,
the grain along the lips rough-cut, unfinished.
I tried to ease Grandfather down,

a sack of bones already gone
before I could run to find my father
sipping coffee on the porch with Meemaw
leaning forward in her rocker when I called.

What God Felt Like
When I Was Twelve

Uncle Sid told me they tore the flesh
from a horse thief near Lubbock in 1880,
gut-cut him and tugged intestines out,
a magician's trick—bandanas knotted
and drawn from a sleeve while the horse thief

howled. Quaker women near a buggy screamed.
Three times they wrapped the string of guts
around the outhouse near the jail.
Three hundred miles from Santa Fe or Dallas,
these arid plains could starve a family,

stranded. *Don't mess with my mount,* even friends
told friends, sunburned in spite of Stetsons
or straw hats. A horse was a Bible, survival,
god. A man was no better than his word,
which carried as far as pistol lead,

echoes not even cactus grew. Old Uncle Sid
lashed me with his eyes and took the reins,
his best palomino sweaty. He made me unsaddle
and brush the stallion, while the horse bent down
and nuzzled the trough for water, turning,

blowing spray in my face, baptism of holy oats
that choked me, sweat and sprinkled face
like a call from God—a golden horse I stole
and rode, and Uncle Sid's gloved fist
thumping like mercy on my skull.

Words I Looked Up in World War Two

Migraine takes her away,
Grandmother said when Aunt Marge
shuddered and fell, eyes rolling back,
like Orphan Annie's. In Sunday school,
I feared a demon had her. *Migraine*

seemed like *Mammon, Satan.*
Epilepsy, my daddy called it,
another word to learn.
I watched her writhe, white-faced.
When we hugged, I laid on hands.

Aunt Marge was a tough one,
a big-boned laughing girl I loved,
always tickling us, pulling dimes
from behind our ears, rare
as dollars before Pearl Harbor.

Long-haired and lovely, she taught us
cards and hide-and-seek and horse,
and turned eighteen and enlisted.
My brother was ten with a temper,
kicked her once when she won.

I dragged him kicking
and scratching behind the barn
and taught him how to lose.
She passed the physical by lying,
handsome in Marine Corps blues.

Her troop ship burned off Okinawa.
I was fourteen by then, and big,
but enlistment sergeants led me out
to the sidewalk, patting my shoulders,
saying, *Don't worry, it's okay,*

the war's almost won. They'd seen
so many grieving, needing to kill
to cope—maybe saw my jaw too tight,
the eyes too puffy, the nicks
where I tried to shave.

Uncle Bob and the Art of Taxidermy

His cabin was a mansion of games, pool tables
and decks of solitaire. That shack
balanced on a mountain of boulders,
buried by snow in the San Juan.
Big man with a beard and eye patch,
he stuffed illegal bucks and wolves

for tourists he despised. When they left,
he slammed the door behind him.
He growled as if he hated nephews

but slipped me bubblegum and winked,
taught me to hold my tongue and listen to hawks
and elk on mountains a mile away. Bob lived alone
with his rifle and knives. His wife had died
in Houston traffic. I knew her name,

the names of dead cousins. At night,
stuffing another head, he swore the best way
was never to marry, to travel light,
to climb steep cliffs and tunnel in.

I think he hoped boulders would crash on him
like Samson, wanting no car horns,
no tons of burning metal, only hawks
and bald eagles, the clicking of aspen,
and after dark, paws crunching on shale,
the muffled breath of a bear.

Packing Parachutes in Flight School

We beat each other senseless in football
and boxing, swimming in flight suits
before we soloed. Five resigned
after their first flights, nervous
or breakfast on the canopy. By frost,
most soloed, flew to Florida and back
alone, packed our own parachutes

to feel how it's done, our necks
depending on slender nylon cords.
Weekends, we cruised for Georgia girls
who trained us to love buttered grits
and yams, dancing to Johnny Mathis
who swore we'd be true until the twelfth
of never. One noon, a boy in our class

crash-landed, trailing smoke—Joe,
somebody said—too low to bail out,
smoke billowing, wing clipping
the pine trees and flipping, a fireball
for a thousand yards, some of us
running toward the wreckage
until the captain called us back.

Before Flying Off to War

Before war, practice alms. Diplomas, awards
in fancy frames, anything with your name engraved,
give up. Take trophies to kids on the street
too skinny to win. Give away your coat,

both coats. Stock the pantry for your wife,
but haul your tools to a school, slum-side of town,
let them pick crowbars and hammers, drills, your awl,
your favorite cross saw. Donate your second car

to the Salvation Army, the March of Dimes—
it doesn't matter, and give them snow tires
you saved for a dazzling trip to Alaska.
Throw in the pup tent, your Boy Scout badges,

Grandfather's elk heads in the attic.
Give all black Bibles away but one. No,
hold nothing back. Even Saigon has chaplains.
Give up your wife, both children. Silently say goodbye

to Mother, Father far away. Haul out the trunk
and dump whatever's left. Drag it outside.
A truck from the Foundation for the Blind
comes by on Fridays. By Friday, you'll be gone.

PART 3

Taking the
Keys Away

Taking the Keys Away

Daddy at the wheel is dangerous,
we finally had to admit—Daddy,
who drove tanks for Patton,
directed fire at steel,
at walls a thousand years old,

at trucks with a dozen boys.
Now, for the fourth time,
he straddled a curb, backing up

almost over a mailman, who leaped aside
in time, with his hands out,
watching his pushcart crushed.
What if tomorrow it's a boy on a bike,
a widow walking her dog,

a toddler? How to tell a tank commander
with white hair, *Please give us the keys?*
How to sit down by Father and say,

You're grounded? He doesn't lose
the remote control more than once
a program. Calls the dog the wrong name
often, but even the dog
comes gladly, happy for his hand.

The War in Bosnia,
the Beach at Kitty Hawk

Black, or mother-of-pearl, they snag on sand,
stranded till seagulls pick them clean.
We find seashells on restaurant walls
and sold as souvenirs, even above commodes,

glue-gunned to silk and plastic flowers
wrapped into wreaths, clams and conchs
washed up at Kitty Hawk. We stroll packed sand,
bending to pick pink shells with granddaughters.

Starfish tumble ashore in bubbles
washing our socks with salt. Skipping,
our granddaughters save sand dollars,
moonsnails, hopping when waves ebb out

and scatter shells they bend to pick,
and squeal when waves rush back
and splash their rubber boots.
Decades ago, I combed a barbed-wire beach

for shells as souvenirs to send our son,
nothing else like war in Vietnam that night
but guards with M16s. Tonight,
our son in Bosnia flies an Apache gunship,

patrolling more than ocean, firefights
he can't stop. I wonder if Orville and Wilbur
thought about bombs and rockets
when they launched facedown

a mile from here. Now, near Kitty Hawk,
my wife and I sip coffee on the condo's deck,
granddaughters finally asleep.
We face the east where our son flies

thousands of stars from here,
hot coffee cooling as we sip,
nothing to see but miles of dark
and white caps crashing down.

The Gulls of Kitty Hawk

Gulls swoop and glide,
angels guarding sea breeze, sand and stars.
Gulls brood and stare over foam
and worship waves forever rolling.
They roost on bells of swaying buoys,
balanced on the wash and roar of waves,
the ebb and flow of boats.

Grandchildren in the Maritime Museum

In a hall of coastal birds airborne on wires
in seaside, diorama skies,
our granddaughter watched them all,
believing those stuffed owls would wink,
their cartoon eyes soon blink.
Hands on her knees, she stared at possums

that held their breath, and natty,
stiff raccoons with bandit eyes.
Leaning, she waved at eagles and hawks
with rubber snakes clutched tight,
and painted pelicans that never dived.
At a roped-off marsh of splendid, pink flamingos,

our grandchild slowly raised one foot,
like one of the birds. She pursed her lips
to make a flamingo beak, balanced
like part of the flock on the edge of wonder.
This child of flat horizons on the plains
gazed at displays of mammals and birds

like Oz and Disney World, believing it all,
the backdrop spotlights bouncing gold
and rosy on her face, making her pink cheeks shine.
She heard a squeal of joy down the hall
and ran to the main aquarium,
tall panels where girls and boys

watched sea bass wide enough for saddles,
dolphins with silver-dollar eyes.
Schools of tuna glided past under tons
of aquarium ocean, even nurse sharks
harmless as dachshunds. Turtles
big as golf carts paddled by—

thousands of rays and reef fish
drifting, waving wide fins
at children giddy to see them all,
dashing from panel to panel,
shouting in whispers, *Look! Look!*
pressing their hands and noses to the glass.

That Night and Others Like It

Round like wagon wheels out of Columbus,
the moon rose orange and massive over the plains,
Comanche moon, moon of ten thousand years of people
huddled and wondering, drawing models of the moon.
So many pictographs, crescents and bulging bellies,

arrowheads and antelopes and bears. Anything
killable, ready to be skinned and lived in, eaten
or worn—deer and bison, woolly mammoths,
the shaggy shawls of wolves and necklaces of teeth.
In 1880, my great-greats wobbled down from Ohio,

following signs of coyotes and God's own book of stars.
Wolves sniffed their cows at night, red eyes
flashing in campfires. This warped and split-wood wheel
is all we own, their clock and trunk of treasures
burned to ashes, house fire they survived without albums,

not even a family Bible. Their moon was a huge, blank ball
pockmarked over Lubbock. Decades later, my buddy Duke
hopped there, lifted rocks and practiced golf swings,
leaving a flag, moon rover with dented piano-wire tires.
When Great-grandmother climbed down on this dirt,

the town was nothing, not even shacks, only buffalo grass
and a canyon where they watered cattle near cliffs
with pictographs, and pitched their tent, night coming on,
coyotes howling at wagons and an orange moon
looming across a thousand miles.

Months of Butterrum

Grandmother smelled like rum,
her own Lifesaver. She swayed us
on her knees and whispered secrets—

*Even the butter in butterrum
is fake. But taste it,* she urged
and hugged us. Grandmother's tongue

spun mysteries, those bears
and Goldilocks, the big bad wolf.
She taught us how cooks up in Jersey

make candy from embers, how a pot
boils sugar and water to rum.
She slid Lifesavers like wafers

between our lips, holy snacks
at nap time in her house.
We sucked butterrum like honey

while Grandmother rocked us
and read from a book on her lap—
Daniel in the lions' den, Samson

with fists full of honey from lions.
We stroked the bouncing pouch
of her throat, touching the hot

vibrato of her voice box.
Whenever Grandmother coughed,
she turned us away, chuckling,

trying to hide the blood spots
of her handkerchief,
the mystery of her lungs.

Giving Time to the Dirt in Rows

My wife framed a poster decades ago,
Take time—picture of a daddy holding a kid.
So I made time for them at baseball games,
before survival training and Saigon.
Down on both knees, I taught our babies
tickle and horsy rides, caught all three kids
with the same oiled catcher's mitt,

then waved them away on planes. Berries and beans
sustain us, now that our children have gone—
and okra so slick why bother to chew,
just swallow. There's work in digging our own
potatoes—never mind the worms, dirt
under the nails. It's grace, no matter how high
the water bill, how many bushels we reap.

All that crawling around between rows
takes time, squatting like ducks hunting for bugs,
turning flab into muscle, to tighter skin
and bone. Years ago, each child turned back
and waved—memories we keep like nights
in Montana, blessings no one could earn,
like potatoes, berries, and beans.

Uncle Earl's Last Ride in Dallas

Uncle Earl's blue suit hung like a rustler's,
four pairs of boots lined up like a posse's
in the closet. We did what we must
with a will's stipulation—Levi's
and long-sleeved shirt unbuttoned,
his best beaver Stetson, back brim cut flush

to let his head lie flat. A chaw of Red Man
in his jaws, stitched tight and natural,
except no ooze, no chewing. Dress boots
were under there somewhere, although
no coffin would show them, polished or not.
But when they rolled the casket in, we heard

the jangle of spurs, muffled by the fluff
and satin. Old Earl would have been the first
to chortle, the way he hobbled off with his hat,
gored by the only bull to toss him in years,
a glove holding his ribs to hide the blood,
as if patting his chest pocket for a smoke.

Fencing the Hardpan

Under packed dirt, locked under chalky mud,
caliche shudders and gives way, the white
and gritty hardpan of the plains. Each bite
of posthole diggers drops a hollow thud,

then *thunk* when the hole goes deep. A foot,
sometimes three feet down into tight topsoil,
digging goes easy. Who could believe this hot
and dusty desert was a sea, crushed underfoot

millions of years before Noah? Here sponges bloated,
fat on easy plankton, and coral after long life
died in colonies of shells too small to find,
falling to mush of sandy mud, floating

more softly than leaves in a breeze on a lake.
How many tons of chalky carbonate to an acre,
how many shells in each digger I lift and shake?
Three feet will do, or four for corner stakes,

posts sunk in centuries and packed to hold
four rolls of barbed wires in the wind.
Now let them come, the dumb and bulky steers
content to graze, the awkward long-legged foals

turned loose, once-playful clumsy calves
walleyed and bawling for mamas, cut
and turned loose to boredom and pleasures of gut
with older steers in green pastures,

let them eat. What drives us all
is hunger for God or fodder, pain in the heart
or the scrotum, ovary and thumb squeezing hard
to make an egg or fence, a fresh start

on limited range under heaven, a home,
a wild child clapping and laughing, a calf
bowed in the August heat over chaff,
grazing the grass of bonemeal and loam.

On the Porch Swing at Dawn

Beans of Costa Rica heat my tongue,
arabica coffee dark as the backyard,
without stars. My wife sleeps in today,

at last, after the long ride back.
Cold comfort that ice may thaw today,
still far below freezing. Steam rises,

but with gloves I don't feel the mug.
A thousand miles away, our granddaughter's warm,
the hospital always warm. There,

it's already five, night nurses high on coffee
about to go out to their cars, to whatever problems
or rewards they'll find at home.

When I rock, chains creak, and frozen fog
sloughs off. Fresh gourmet beans and mugs,
a gift from her at Christmas. She knows

Mamaw and Pop rock softly at dawn and sip.
I watch for stars, for any signs of dawn.
I believe the moon and stars are there

past the overcast. I believe in spite of drifts
and bridges, almost impassable, dangerously iced,
nurses keep watch and hover in her room.

A Clown Fired from a Cannon

Sleet taps the screens, bounces like pellets
dipped in buttermilk by clowns, shot at a crowd
with popguns. On the porch, bundled up,
I watch the clouds for signs, a hint of angels.

My luck again, two-fisted braggart on the ropes.
I fold, unlucky in cards, starving for faith.
No sense in betting daily food on these. Crumbs,
I'd stoop for crumbs. Go on, kick me with doubt,

I'll bite like a bulldog, I'm foaming,
I won't let go. Lately, I've taken to the streets,
trotting after cars, barking, nipping bumpers
and stumbling, a hound with no master,
        hoping for handouts,

mad-dog dreamer pretending to be sane. I need only
a bone of faith—not a flash streaking through heaven,
power swished fiercely inside the clouds—
but even a whisper, more like a shock than a rainbow.

Let it linger in the brain, an after-image,
synapses snapping for hours like a clown
fired from a cannon to a net flimsy as faith,
echoes from outer space, *over*, *over.*

After Fires in Montana

Fire blackened every hearth for miles
but Uncle Herb's lodge in Montana,
dozens of neighbors and strangers in beds
and sleeping bags. Our daughter thought it a party,

but not our girl-shy boys, who would rather fish
and watch grizzlies. They watched the clock,
the swinging gong Uncle Herb shipped home from Germany.
Every hour, I let them out to sniff the smoke.

The radio warned the winds might shift,
trees dry as beef jerky, the roads still blocked.
Cougars and bears were out there, who knows where,
the ones not burned. Uncle Herb's voice boomed

Next twelve, and neighbors checked their numbers,
leaned back or wedged their way to the dining hall,
past strangers who nodded, others in the lobby
counting their children again or cupping palms

to their ears to hear, a dozen cell phones
but relay towers down, stranded another night,
no danger of starving with a basement of kegs
and a smokehouse. After the waiters ate

and tourists put away their phones and shrugged,
bald Uncle Herb climbed up on the counter,
whistling, waving his Smoky the Bear hat
and harmonica, calling us all to song.

PART 4

October
Compost

Downhill to Granddaddy's Barn

Pulling the wagon downhill by hand,
Granddaddy turned the tongue on the slope
to make the left front bump,

and the whole tree shuddered.
Pecans clattered like a hailstorm,
rattling on the wagon and ground.

His butt leaned back, slid down to the hitch
and he sighed, shaking his head
as if a little work was too much.

When I was a boy, I saw him lift a calf
to its mother, his big arms bulging.
The Angus was thicker than him,

but gentle, three-legged and healing
after gangrene. He sawed off
the mangled leg about to burst,

and nursed the bull calf like a dog.
Poor devil, he called it. He waited
in the barn till the cow took it back.

Now, he waited while I jogged uphill
from the barn, his red face wet, hat off,
suspenders loose and white hair

matted on his brow. *It's downhill all the way,*
he said and pointed at the barn,
and I can't stop it. We turned it

together, guiding between trees
a thousand yards down toward the barn,
pecan shells crunching under tires,

Granddaddy tight-lipped, both of us
holding the load with shoulders and butts
to the wagon, trying to hold it back.

The Rockies, Tooth and Claw

Dawn, a dozen finches at the feeder,
a Steller's jay hop-hopping to the trough
Goliath-like to drive them off. Go,
hairy woodpecker waking my wife,

bang the wall, it's dawn. Black squirrel
with trickster's ears, climb down,
teeth first, and spook the goldfinch twins.
I need rich yellow swirls. Hummers, come,

the bottle's full. Suck sugar water hung here
just for you after thousands of miles
on the flyway. Graze, mule deer,
drop your ticks. My slopes are yours

and elks' more often than they're mine.
Peck, robins, gobble all that fall,
plump deer ticks gorged with blood.
Come, hungry coyotes, I won't shoot.

Come, frisky town dogs
following a scent too far uphill,
since training and gates can't stop you.
Come, cougars, dinner's here.

A Brief Familiar Story of Winter

Ample as bears, winter sleeps
where it falls. Forget the sun,
the snowpacked meadows
scattered with diamonds,
the glazed oaks stiff—one breath,

then another, dreaming of summer.
In time, the deepest storms
pick up their beds—pine needles
stacked under drifts.
Up with the bears, chinook wind

shakes the piñons, draining snow
like a swamp, one crystal trickle
into another, melting a mile of ice
a month, then tumbling, rushing
in swift, white-churning floods.

My Wife's First Day of Class

I stopped by during break. *Yes,*
she whispered, *yes,* and shoved me
back to work. All morning, my wife watched
tiny scissors cut, and she was a kid again,
how lucky could a teacher be? Her tongue
tasted sweet like her lipstick

after that first class. She shrugged,
she couldn't help it: the smell of paste
and crayons was enough. Her twenty children
turned pink papers around and upside down
and cut, and stubby fists colored,
making Valentines for months later.

Twenty first-grade tongues twisted out
and around and licked to teach
their clumsy scissors how to snip.
She watched those agile tongues contort,
and she was a child again, cutting sails
to make a boat, her own big teacher's tongue

turning somersaults along her lips,
licking her lipstick. *Yes,*
she whispered, she loved it,
needed children of her own, twins
to start with, or triplets,
something we could talk about tonight.

Angelica's Banjo and Karate

Aunt Angie taught karate and banjo at the mall
after her last boy left for boot camp.
Firemen signed up when she flipped the big one
off the platform near the fountain,

a tag-team match of music and self-defense.
Old Aunt Mary named her baby Angelica,
the first baby born on the plains after Pearl Harbor.
Aunt Angie raised five boys, marines like their father,

a banjo the last thing she tried to stop crying
after Uncle Eddy stepped on a mine outside Da Nang.
A banjo's twang and jangle made any blood dance,
too busy listening to brood. So she married a marine,

what else? Aunt Angie had boxed since high school,
thrown the discus farther than most boys. Karate was easy
after the pain of babies with broad shoulders—
no morphine, but Eddy was there in the delivery room

four times out of five. Her first day at the mall,
Aunt Angie and I played "Dueling Banjos"
faster than local girls could dance. Then
she circled the college coach and dumped him,

dumped him five more times for a crowd of hundreds.
Off-duty cops signed up for karate and banjo,
the whole package, young couples who hoped
they could save each other, worried mothers in sweats

who knew about drugs and teenage rage
like dolphins with babies caught in tuna nets, boys
in the crowd who waved their fists with dollars
for karate, almost ready for the marines.

Some Days Nothing Can Save Us

Once, when our son was four,
playing with cousins, he slammed
and stumbled into the house,
crying as if smashed by a rock.

Older kids told why, led us
to a dumpster in the alley
a few doors down. All had gone
exploring, peeking at trash
to see what treasures

neighbors had thrown away. Sometimes,
a day brings games and baubles;
sometimes, bricks and blood.
The shock of what Charles saw
was a fact I never learned
until Saigon, that some days

nothing can save us. Some fool
had killed blind kittens with a stone,
and for weeks they clawed
in his mind at night, kitten fur
and blood and bile, little teeth
like zippers that couldn't close.

Black as the Plains Out There

High Lonesome tipped back his hat
and his horses snorted. Maybelle nodded,
her teacher's smile a wild azalea
in miles of cactus. My uncle's buckboard

groaned to a stop, in town for flour
and grease and beans. All that, decades ago,
before he taught me how to cowboy. Five summers
we broke broncs, patched fences cut by hunters,

shot coyotes hobbling and starved.
He never married after Maybelle died,
no one to carry on the herd but me, a summer nephew.
Uncle Rollie taught me to rope and brand,

leap back when the calf jumped up.
He taught me to shoot, a mile-long whine
across a mile of pasture. His ribs were gaunt
as an old bull's, alone on an August range.

While I flew back from Vietnam, he died.
His saddles and gates were still the same.
My wife and I moved out to the ranch,
wild windmills whirring, the same bad drought.

Our children left home years ago,
leaving us rocking at night under stars,
far from them all, from the wall in Washington
where Don and Kelly and Harper's names

are carved in granite black as the plains
out there—no moon, tonight, no one but us
to hear the coyotes, the squeal of a field mouse
caught by an owl, flapping back to the barn.

The Winter of Desert Storm

Our grandchild turned five on an Army post
under the roar of fighters training hard
for combat. My wife and I watched her coast,
granddaughter kicking wildly on a swing.

Before our son flew off to Desert Storm,
he drove us to posts of the Civil War,
past the prison cell of Jefferson Davis.

How safe it must have seemed in 1865, no war,
no killing anymore. Redcoats had dug pits
two centuries ago, and waited with muskets,
soldiers from Liverpool and Leeds on foreign soil.

In 1862 that Yorktown fort's stone walls
were blasted down by cannons. When I flew home
from Vietnam, how simple raising babies seemed,

our boy far from Desert Storm, boisterous in the hall,
inventing chaos in homeroom, his elbow
pumping a joyful noise with his palm
in an armpit till he and his teacher screamed.

On the post, with her daddy gone, I thought of wars
almost forgotten, the long black wall
in Washington, the names I touched last week,
the war on every channel, and our boy overseas.
What could we do but shove his daughter's swing,
the jets so loud she had to shout to sing.

October Compost

Leaf rakes go back, go back and trees give up
more leaves than roots can use. Pack down
the pounds of locust leaves, the aspen gold
and fat catalpa bark. All summer we stacked
the pantry, hauled bushels of ears to neighbors
and the town's food bank. Now come the geese
from Canada, fields with loud flocks

pecking grain and corn. Our yard's a compost.
Bring out pitchforks and garden hose, turn
barrels of garbage for the garden, tumble,
churn it like sauerkraut steamy and damp.
All seasons whisper resurrection.
I need this gray decay. Since March,
I've wrestled bales of barbed wire,

bossed the herds, but fall brings cattle trucks.
Runt calves and old cows ride to slaughter.
Fall feeds the soil, and harvest saves
the stalks as silage to make cold cattle fat.
Fall saves migrating geese from freezing,
leads us to spring, tilling the earth
till springer cows give birth.

Christ saves us from decay
we're destined for. Soon enough, we'll shove
wheelbarrows of dark October compost
and watch the dry dirt bulge, mulch of worms
and beetles making debris a kingdom.
Come, shirtsleeve months, come
bawling calves cavorting in corrals.

A Little World Made Cunningly

Carl Sagan thought the billions and billions of stars
the Hubble telescope saw were possibly a molecule
inside a massive universe whose size we can't imagine.
But (forefinger up)—what if that monstrosity

is only an atom of another universe more vast?
What a Brobdingnag of galaxies the final big-bang size
would be—unless *final* limits the infinite too much
for words. I remember pictures of me as a toddler

when my mother and father were the world.
Flip the Hubble, focus on a mote of dust
on anyone's nose, a molecule: inside,
another universe, a billion light years wide.

Think of a billion molecules in the legs
of each of us, each with a billion . . . and so on.
Imagine a minuscule Lilliputian kid inside a galaxy
inside your own left eye, skipping along

to a candy store with a dime. Drops it, dusts it off.
Each dust mote thousands of molecules across,
each tiny atom a cosmos. Maybe it doesn't matter,
if we're helpless, and maybe we'll never know.

No wonder when I sat with Mother for hours
between nurses' rounds, I had no love of knowledge,
the last thing on my mind astronomy.
When she opened her eyes her last long night,

I didn't wonder how many billions of galactic,
giddy girls might be in tiny high schools
inside her, in every atom of cancer, didn't ponder
how many angels danced on her IV needle.

I wanted only one to give comfort, more relief
than I'd ever give when every second seemed
like a world without end, and every year
with that woman who bore me was too brief.

After the Mad Songs of Saigon

Squeezing a half-eaten peach,
I rub the other palm
along the saddle horn,
wrap the reins around it twice,
lean back and slide the rifle out.
I tap the stallion's neck

and give the peach. He twists,
nibbles and swallows,
and his whole neck quivers.
He knows the crack
a rifle makes, and waits.

This won't disturb the universe,
a few ounces into the heart
of a big cat sleeping it off.
That lamb would have died
hereafter, but it was mine,

mine, even the grass and cactus
by that cave with a cougar's tail.
I watch it twitch. Again, like nights
in jungles outside Saigon,
I hear mosquitoes sing.

Finding My Father's Hands in Midlife

My wife keeps hearth and kitchen clean,
bills tallied and guests invited back.
What's a grandfather for?—fists scarred
and knuckles stiff, like my father's,
steers in our Texas pastures fat

and horses saddled, but no sons home.
We raised four kids who married
and moved away, and now as a daddy I'm broke,
no easy advice like cash to wave around.
I taught them to ride and rope,

toss loops and take sick cattle down,
to brand and release wild calves.
The ranch made money in spite of drought
and hours without us, ball games
and camping trips, teenage rage

and car wrecks, the highs and lows
of seasons gone before I learned to let go.
Now, toddlers crawl from cars and waddle
to my arms, our children and in-laws
with babies they bring back. I spend all I own

giving horsy rides and candy, learning
by crawling how to grandfather—any games
they want to play, down on my knees
and knuckles under eight grandchildren
tugging and hugging, showing me how to go.

The Women under Rubens' Thumb

All Rubens loved, they scoffed, was fat flesh
he pinched pink. Under his thumb,
burnt umber smudged over ear lobes
and buttocks. If models blushed,
he loved them, indecencies of silks
and brush. When the rich went to heaven

in his canvas, some saucy goddess
exposed herself, count on it, chin turned
indifferently toward the court, arms raised
behind her neck. They said he made
a mockery of myths, a shamble of classics.
He needed patrons bad-tempered and vain,

but painted legends to mock them,
big-loined and blonde, lips so wet
they glistened. Yes, he made flesh
magnificent, no way to save it,
nothing to do but capture it in oils.
Named after Peter and Paul,

the main apostles, Rubens knew
what men growing old wanted most,
the same as him. When he died
in his sixties, his wife
was carrying another child. They said
he never corrected, so arrogant

he touched a lip or eyelash quickly
and went on, a flushed model hot
and hungry by windows he kept locked,
shouting at her, *No breeze,*
no eating until I'm done. But who
would make the cross be lifted

more than once? Watch his Madonna,
almost reluctant to suckle her chubby child,
sensing his quick descent into manhood.

Consider his dying Christ in Antwerp,
the agony enough without saying,
Wait, let's do that again.

PART 5

Out past
the Breakers

After His Apache Crashed

Now, out past the breakers, dolphins pass,
dark bodies glistening, arching in perfect curves,
single file like an honor guard. For months
our son's helicopter tracked down the Outer Banks
past Kitty Hawk, back up the coast and home.
Daily he saw them graceful past the breakers,

a mile-long hunting habit. Later, when his crew
went down in Bosnia, we waited by the phone for days,
nothing but scandal on TV, the decline and rise
of stocks, death of a princess and an agéd saint.
This year, we're here to grieve on the beach
of Kill Devil Hill, to watch the dolphins

that never knew our son, that don't honor him at all
in solemn, dignified review. We're here
because they're here, because he said they're here,
and that's enough, that's not nearly enough
to take back with us to the plains where dolphins
and starfish haven't lived for a million years.

Fog on the Outer Banks

Fog rocks us almost to sleep,
waves roll and wash the beach at dawn.
Sipping hot coffee on the deck, we rock
and watch our breath make smoke that drifts
and disappears in mist so dense
we listen for foghorns in the harbor.
My wife drags her moccasins
to stop us, leans out and listens
to the hissing beach. No one seems up
but us, and we're too numb to stroll.

Let snails and starfish crawl,
let jellyfish float up in foam,
conchs and shark pods beached
for the picking. Today at the beach
there's nothing to see but fog
shifting shapes, so we don't focus,
mystery enough to rock and watch it,
letting it come, turning our eyelids
clammy as cobwebs, damp enough
to shiver, coffee already cool
although our full cups slosh.

Lay Down the Battle-Ax, the Halyard

It's done in wonder, like falling on ice
and rising, or finally reaching a high note,
shocked by a noise in the night
that would make white marble ring:

Paul, on Damascus Road, blinded by light,
and seeing. Blind Bartimaeus,
so lightly touched he flinched,
blinking, needing no one to say

That's Him. Lay down the battle-ax
and halyard, the six-mule plow.
Stand still in rocks and weeds,
hardscrabble leached by years of crops,

fire-blackened after harvest.
Take off the cotton sack you've dragged
for decades behind you, loaded with your own
field's stones. Fall down in a row,

in the weeds. Burst clods to dust.
Hold on to nothing you own, let go,
let faith blind as midnight save you,
believing *This is all I need.*

Squall Line at Sixty-Five

Sloshing through sudden bogs,
we leave the trees balled up in the pickup
and retreat to the porch swing,

slinging holy water from our hats.
By tonight, the cloudburst will be gone,
sand almost a crust by dawn.

Two days, even the holes we dug will drain,
foam on the bottom ready for roots.
Now, pears in the pickup tilt

and bend in the wind, and thunder booms.
Cows in the pasture wait, wet muzzles
turned to the wind, eyes almost closed.

The horses are probably downwind by the barn,
hogs clean at last, flicking their snouts
and chomping as if they'll never eat again.

Rocking, we watch the storm and wonder
if grandchildren nine hundred miles away are home
from school, if maybe they'll call tomorrow.

Old Men Are Dreamers

Old men are dreamers, plotting escape all day.
Nights, they're surrounded, millions of stars
that fall. They rise in the dark and feel their way
to chairs. At dawn after coffee, the strong
take walks in malls, or slowly in parks
past wives and toddlers, past boys on bikes, and dogs.

Walking, they argue, cases they seldom lose.
Hackles up like hawks' if they stumble, they refuse
most strangers' hands that lift them anyhow.
A hawk alone knows nothing it couldn't do,
gliding, soaring between thunderclouds,
scrawling its dark, bold name against the blue.

My Father Light as a Boy

Still shaves himself, electric, flat on his back,
chin up to tighten skin on bone. Done,
he holds the shaver on the bed, palm up

like an offering, silver and gold and black.
Decades ago, my father could lift a man-thick log
and heave it over a fence, neck muscles bulging.

Now eighty-five, he's Mother's size, but bald.
He lifts the razor like a crane, underpowered
for such a weight, thin shoulder hinging slowly

toward the tray. I shove up from the chair,
too late. He's there, and turns his palm
to dump it on its side. And being that far there,

he cuts his eyes at me, a sign he'd like to turn.
I lift the bony shoulders and begin to twist,
reach down and turn the gaunt hips bruised

from shots, the knobby knees. He doesn't groan,
won't say a word, biting hard to swallow.
I touch his parchment scalp and rub,

I won't let go. He's staring at the door.
I hear his stomach noise, his breath, his breath.
His eyelids blink, so sticky dry they pop.

Stoking the Logs

Ashes drift down like snow, smoke from the chimney
easy to breathe, split piñon from New Mexico.
Decades of nights come back on the breeze,
coils of memories like DNA—David swinging a rope
from his pony, Cindy in bed with teddy bears

and mumps, teaching bears ballet and tap
on a pillow stage. Now, from rocking chairs,
we watch trees bloom before our eyes through the glass
and weeds turn green. So many miles to Cindy's house,

an ocean between us and Charlie's job, Seville a city
we learned meant *Spain,* light years ago, a town
where exotic others lived. Grandchildren sleep
without us, now, holidays we enjoy

scattered throughout the calendar, any excuse
to call, to hear their voices like windup toys
deep breathing in the receiver, then *I love you
Mamaw and Pop,* or teenage giggles,
granddaughters' call-waiting clicks

and gushy love goodbyes. Pockets of pinesap sizzle
and pop in the fireplace, the bittersweet
aroma of smoke in the room, like our cabin
in the mountains decades ago, our fingers locked
on the sofa, now, big-knuckled and splotched,
a stiff coupling of fingers that still fit.

Stumbling to the Deck at Dawn

March, when Carol and I stumble out to the deck
with iced tea instead of coffee
or find ourselves on the kitchen floor

with coats on in front of an opened freezer door—
we know it's time to go back to cold Montana
to climb, to walk on ice, collapse exhausted

and happy on snowdrifts deep as a house
and breathe that rare and heady air.
We raised babies on the plains,

shared a few swift years of meals with them
and slept, and suddenly they're gone.
Packing for a drive to the mountains,

we think of their first pets, and how they lost them,
the dogs and cats that ran away, the goldfish
and gerbil the older brother flushed down the commode.

Floating on radial tires on the highway,
we know all survivors are Noah, whether we have
two dogs, two cats, or only each other. We blink,

and ten more years are gone. Our cattle graze
and fatten even at night, and nothing, not even power
knocked out by storms, will stop the clock.

Bless Weeds That Bloom in Fall

If lips I've kissed since seventeen are boredom,
give me decades more—her wrinkled skin,
squeeze of her knuckles wearing the same old rings.
Give us Deer Mountain always the same above us,
boulders balanced a thousand years.

We abandoned celibate lives like shedding skin, *I do,*
I do. We drive to the cabin now past the same
mad traffic, gamblers wild on radial tires
turning off at Black Hawk, casino parking lots packed.
In Montana, we rock on the porch at dawn

and watch the same brief, silver showers,
spring snow that flurries and burns away by noon.
We gamble on marriage the old way,
playing the hands we know by heart,
touch familiar as clouds that puff

and bump the Rockies and pass. Bless weeds
that bloom in fall for elk and mule deer
nibbling the same steep slopes, ignoring bears
and slit-eyed cougars lolling in the rocks,
picking which one, which one's next.

Dazzling Montana Dawns

Bring back that rabbit that hopped
over rocks and stopped. It crouched,
not moving even its eyes, as if shifting
might lure the shock of fangs, the least
consequential act in Montana.

Praise hawks and bald eagles,
coyotes, even wolves brought back
to Glacier Park, stalking flocks.
Praise tents for two, green Coleman stoves
and gloves. Bring back a year

that seemed a year, not four brief months
and gone. How quickly we cleared the calendar
and drove back to mountains, buffet style—
a taste of duck, platter heaped
with dazzling mountain dawns.

But we're too stiff for tents
and midnight hikes, so let the rabbit hop,
let buzzards starve, or waddle paunchy
from the bones. Let wolves survive,
let ranchers stalk them all,

let winter come. Let elk herds breed
or freeze, if they must, in drifts.
Let our children take turns
camping Montana mountains, let months
fly by, whatever we can't change.

That Clatter in the Attic

They're back at breakfast,
pattering along the walls
and gnawing, almost chewing through,
beavers of foam board. God,
let the rodents rest. Frenzied,

they nibble. We picture teeth
dripping with deadly microbes
or rabies. Daily, we check the crackers,
the loaf of bread. Last year,

when we closed this mountain cabin,
did they move in? Do they think they own
these walls? What do they think of us

down here with creaking oven doors
and fireplace popping at dawn?
Nights, do our talk and rocking chairs
like alien dangers keep them awake?
Do black, beady eyes bulge wide,
mouse whiskers tense, afraid to twitch?

Clouds Whip By in the Valley

Come feel the sleet in your face, see clouds whip by
in the valley. Crows beat and stagger for trees, pines
flapping like flagpoles. Watch that elk heifer bite
the blue plastic tarp and lift it from the sandpile

by the frozen drive. Watch her chomp and toss it.
Always it settles like a flabby ghost.
She must hope it's covering green grit,
weeds, forbidden grass. She bucks like a colt

and kicks, nipping the blue sheet. Fiercely she shakes
and flings, but it falls and flutters humped
around her hoofs. Watch her twirl and quake,
a tantrum, and lower her hornless skull to butt.

She jerks the blue tarp billowing, a teenager
tossing a bedspread, one corner tucked
at the footboard. Elk cows thick with winter fur
know grass from plastic and graze the stubble like luck,

aware of calves in their bellies kicking,
a pack of coyotes a thousand yards upwind,
and somewhere far off, watching,
a puma lying quietly behind rocks.

Hiking Grizzly Country with Bells

Fawns know to lie still, and grouse chicks
swallow their tongues when grizzlies pass.
We hike with bells and walking sticks,
talking out loud about how nothing's changed,
decades of lightning strikes grown back
as if fire never happened.

Silence can't guarantee safe passage
in this dark forest. Bears, beware,
here come the old folks. Sniff this,
we're the same as forty years ago,
though not as wild. No surprises,
so out of the way for a week.

If you're watching beyond that curve,
go back to gobbling berries.
Our lungs are faithful to fate—
no guns, no tundra to crush,
no reason to fear we're dangerous
to anything but us. In Glacier Park,

Heaven's Peak's a steep cliff
less than 9,000', snowcapped
a mere ten miles away. Gasping,
we hold hands at sixty-five and stare—
even with lightweight boots and packs,
too hard a climb this year.

The Dark, Hollow Halo of Space

Rock of all, my marble, stone
of my tomb and my stairs. More firm
than granite in mountains, you are older
than immortal diamond and gold.

My body is putty, a tiny blue planet
in the dark, hollow halo of space.
Billions of bonfires are specks
in your eye, maker of fabulous galaxies

far from earth, and all burning. My heart
burns slowly, unnoticed, as gold burns,
even novas I've never seen.
I'm numbed by the buckshot of stars,

trillions of tons in each one. When the air
I'm made from is ash, only dust I'll become.
And go when You call, where You are,
stone of my tomb and my stairs.

Jogging at Sixty-Five

Dawn runners call raw wind a bear, bite it
breath by breath until the cold bear roars.
We stumble on ruts frozen stiff as hoes

turned upside down. Sun is a rumor
cirrus clouds pass along like gossip,
gossamer strung from the east like webs.

By sixty, nature gives up on bodies
soft as sand castles after ebb tide.
Puffing, we pump fists doubled on nothing

but lifelines wrinkled when we were born.
Bony legs run to get the old blood
pumping, squeeze, squeeze that blue juice

to our toes, up to skulls of gray hair
sweaty under wool caps flapping our throats.
One old couple could keep this pace all day,

panting around the solid lake to turn
and circle back—shorter to cut across
on ice ten inches thick, but cheating.

Crows hurl themselves from spruce,
cascades of snow we dip through,
not even blinking. Somewhere, a loon

croons its crazy song, and why not.
Our bodies wobble like Apollo 13,
short of oxygen and fuel—makeshift,

but doing what wobbly bodies can do,
the lake a frozen glow that pulls us
like the moon and hurls us home.

About the Author

WALT MCDONALD is the author of nineteen collections of poetry and one book of fiction. More than 2,200 of his poems have been published in journals and magazines, including *The American Scholar, The Atlantic Monthly, Boston Review, First Things, New York Review of Books, JAMA (Journal of the American Medical Association), London Review of Books, The Nation, The New Criterion, Poetry,* and *The Sewanee Review.* McDonald served as Texas Poet Laureate in 2001, and as poetry editor for Texas Tech University Press from 1975 to 1995. He retired in May 2002 as Paul Whitfield Horn Professor of English and Poet in Residence at Texas Tech University.